Christmas P(

25 Days of Bible Study

by Sarah Geringer

Copyright 2017 Sarah Geringer

For my family
and for God's glory

Acknowledgments

Thanks to those who have encouraged me on my writing journey: Chris Becker, Chris Warren, Pastor Mark Martin, and members of the Heartland Writers Guild. Your kindness and support has inspired me so many times when I felt like giving up.

Thanks go to my beta readers, who are friends from school, church, Bible studies, my workplace, and my community. I deeply appreciate your insight and assistance in spreading peace to other moms.

Thanks to Liz Schulte, whose presentation at the 2016 All Write Now! Conference sparked the process of writing my first e-book.

Thanks to Michael Hyatt, Jeff Goins, Tim Grahl, Chandler Bolt, and Sarah Mae for your online training and e-books which have powerfully shaped my writing career. I haven't met you yet, but I count you as my mentors.

Thanks to my husband and children for your patience, support, and understanding as I traded many hours of family time for writing time. I love you with all my heart and hope we enjoy many more peaceful Christmases together.

Above all, thanks go to my Prince of Peace, the One who deserves all the glory.

Table of Contents

Welcome to Peace

The peace of God, which transcends all understanding,
will guard your hearts and your minds in Christ Jesus.
Philippians 4:7

Christmas peace is possible.

But it is only possible with Jesus.

He is the Prince of Peace, the one who gave us peace as a Christmas gift.

When the angels announced his birth, they first praised God. Then they sang,

And on earth, peace to those on whom his favor rests. Luke 2:14

Peace was God's gift to the shepherds that night and to all who believe in Jesus as their Savior now.

God knows we need peace. We are separated from him by sin.

Jesus is God's peace offering to us, his gift of forgiveness and grace. We can have peace with God through Jesus' birth, death, and resurrection.

On the night before his crucifixion, Jesus said to his disciples,

Peace I leave with you; my peace I give you.
I do not give to you as the world gives.
Do not let your hearts be troubled and do not be afraid.
John 14:27

We need his peace in the bustle of busy December.

Like Martha in Luke 10, we are distracted by all the preparations:

- decorating our homes
- shopping for groceries and gifts
- baking and cooking special food
- wrapping all the gifts
- cleaning all the extra messes

Looking at that list makes my heart race—but I've plodded through that list every year I've been a mom.

Like Martha, I have been worried and upset about how much work is to be done in preparation for Christmas. I wanted picture-perfect memories of Christmas with my family. For many years, my peace got lost in the pursuit of perfection.

By sitting at Jesus' feet like Mary, I found the peace I needed. You can find this peace too. In the next 25 days, we will spend 15 minutes each day walking through this process of finding Christmas peace:

- When I set aside time each day for God's word, I find peace.
- When I plan ahead for the next day, I find peace.
- When I focus on making memories with my family, I find peace.
- When I lower my expectations for a perfect holiday, I find peace.
- When I choose to serve others at Christmas, I find peace.
- When I reflect on God's goodness to me in the past year, I find peace.

I invite you on a journey of peace this Christmas. We will start with finding peace in our own hearts and gradually move outward to sharing peace with others.

For even more Christmas peace, sign up for free study materials, printables and videos in the pink box at **sarahgeringer.com.**

Week 1: Peace in my Heart

A heart at peace
gives life
to the body.
Proverbs 14:30

Day 1: Peace with God

Therefore, since we have been justified through faith,
we have peace with God through our Lord Jesus Christ.
Romans 5:1

I find peace with God because of who he is.

He is high above me, watching over me, yet he is near. He is holy, good, and loving. He is trustworthy. He is all-powerful, all-wise, all-knowing, all-seeing.

He shines his searchlight on my heart, examining my motives and my ways. He sees all my hidden vices—the silent criticism, the hatred, the lashing out. The snarky comments never voiced. The unforgiveness. The brokenness, anxiety, inadequacy. He sees it all.

Yet he loves me anyway. God calls me his own. I am his precious daughter, just like my young daughter is to me. No one else on earth loves her the way I do. I treasure her smile, her eyelashes, her sweet hugs, her artistic talent, her silly fun, her singing voice. I see the baby, girl, and future woman all wrapped up together in her innocent eyes. My love for her is fierce, deep, and everlasting. She is pure joy to my heart.

That's how God sees me. I am *more* precious to him than my daughter is to me. In my relationship to her, I catch a glimpse of how he loves me.

How he takes delight in me, even though I'm not fully mature, even though earlier today I yelled at him and pouted when I didn't get what I want.

He doesn't mind when my hair is unruly or when I have a tomato sauce stain on my shirt. He always sees past the imperfections and treasures my inner beauty.

9

His greatest joy of the day is when I run to him, lay in his lap, and take comfort in his embrace. He puts his hand on my head and whispers a blessing over me, just as I do with my daughter at bedtime. He adores me.

I didn't always see God that way. Since my parents divorced when I was young, I had a hard time trusting my father, men in general, and God too. I saw God as powerful and majestic, a mighty ruler, one to be awed and revered. Distant.

I wasn't close to God until I was a troubled teen and called out to God for help. He rescued me from my depression, and I came to know Jesus as my friend. Through Jesus, I began to experience peace with God.

For a long time, I let obstacles get in the way. In college, I struggled with guilt over rebellion...surely God didn't love me as much. As a mom of three little ones, I struggled with guilt over lack of quiet time...surely God thought I should be more spiritual. In times of financial struggle, I felt shame...surely God looked down on me.

Yet in my worst trials, I clung to my faith, and the only place I found peace in the storms was at Jesus' feet. Pouring out raw and ugly prayers. Searching his word for encouragement. Reaching out to my church family for support. Sitting still and knowing he is in control.

I found peace with God in my trials. I knew he loved me and believed in me. He didn't hold anything against me. He simply wanted me to come to him.

I found peace with God by being totally honest in our conversations. By treating him like a friend—taking turns listening and talking, sharing everyday moments with him, laughing with him.

Because Romans 5:1 says I'm forgiven, that I have been justified through faith, I have peace with God. My heart is at peace knowing no more obstacles stand between us.

Have you found peace with God in your own story?

Day 1 Questions for Study and Reflection:

Read Psalm 46. When you are still before God, reflecting on who he is, which attributes in this psalm bring peace to your heart?

REFUGE, STRENGTH, Ever-present help in trouble. God
is WITH HER. God will HELP HER at the break of day.
The God of Jacob is our FORTRESS.

What obstacles from your past block your peace with God?

My insecurity and the self-doubt from those years of being
bullied - it makes me strive for approval, fear being rejected,
stay anxious about what people are thinking instead of resting in
the
How does your relationship with your children reflect the way
God loves you?

I see them for who they will be for all of their approval
potential. I see them through eyes of love. I have
great hope for them. I don't look at them through their past
failures

Read Romans 5:1-11. How is peace with God the Father possible only through Jesus?

¹ we have been JUSTIFIED through FAITH,
we have PEACE with God through JESUS
CHRIST, through whom we have GAINED
ACCESS by FAITH into this GRACE
in which we now STAND. And we BOAST
in the HOPE of the Glory of GOD. ⁹ Since
we have now been JUSTIFIED by HIS BLOOD,
how much more shall we be SAVED from
God's wrath through him! ¹⁰ We were RECONCILED
to him through the DEATH of his SON.

Day 2: Peace with Myself

I praise you because I am fearfully and wonderfully made.
Psalm 139:14

For the longest time, we had no full-length mirror in our home, and that was just fine with me.

During the years without a full-length mirror I had my three babies. I gained the most weight with my third pregnancy because I overate during stressful circumstances. The bathroom scale told me I was at my biggest weight in years, but since I couldn't see anything below my shoulders in the bathroom mirror, I was in denial.

One day about a year after my third child was born, I stood in line at a mall restaurant with floor-to-ceiling mirrors. I glimpsed an overweight woman in the mirrors and realized she was me. I couldn't hide from the 35 extra pounds I was carrying. The truth glared at me under fluorescent lighting. My denial was blown.

I began the challenging process of working toward a healthy weight. My biggest challenge, however, was not dealing with sore muscles or cutting back on chocolate—it was resisting the temptation to condemn myself, to slip into self-hatred.

I started avoiding mirrors as an overweight teen. I binged because I was depressed, then I gained weight, then I became more depressed, binged again, and the cycle repeated. I didn't want to face the truth I saw in mirrors, so I wore huge, baggy clothing. No matter how hard I tried to hide, I still heard inner voices of condemnation: You're ugly. You're fat. You don't deserve love.

Those painful words held me in bondage as a teen. I worked hard to resist their power as an adult.

I found comfort in Psalm 139, which I consider my love letter from God.

He discerns my going out and my lying down—He knows everything about me.

He created my inmost being and knit me together—He cares lovingly for me.

All the days ordained for me were written in his book—He created me with purpose.

In my process of shedding weight and making healthy choices, I steeped myself in these passages about God's love. God's Word silenced my internal voices of condemnation with his powerful truth.

About a year after the mall mirror incident, we installed a full-length mirror in our master bathroom. I took a moment to look over my body one day after stepping out of the shower.

It wasn't perfect. Every mom knows her body changes after children are born. My stretch marks were in plain sight, along with my cellulite. I felt the downward pull of condemnation tempting me.

But God prompted me, "Look at what is good." I focused on what I do like about my body, the body God gave me. The facial features he chose for me, the overall body shape he designed.

I thought of his words—I am fearfully and wonderfully made.

And for the first time in my life, I stood naked in front of a mirror, and agreed with God that my body is good, just the way it is.

The peace I found with myself that day was powerful. It changed the way I talk to myself. It changed the way I talk about myself when I'm in public. I no longer tear myself down, internally or externally.

I have peace with myself because I am precious to God. Dear friend, you are precious to him as well!

Day 2 Questions for Study and Reflection:

Read Psalm 139 slowly and carefully, as if it is God's love letter to you. What do you learn about God from this psalm? About yourself?

What can you do differently next time you hear inner voices of condemnation?

List three things about your body that you like.

Be brave: stand naked in front of a full-length mirror and study your body as if you were taking in a masterpiece of art. What do you see that is fearfully and wonderfully made?

Day 3: Peaceful Expectations

The mind governed by the Spirit is life and peace.
Romans 8:6

What are your expectations in this Christmas season?

Maybe you are a Pinterest fan, studying hundreds of ideas for the perfect party. A planner at heart, you aim for perfection.

Maybe you pretend nothing bad will happen and you skate on the surface of Christmas. A little girl at heart, you hope for no conflict.

Maybe you are a closet Grinch, going along with the festivities for the sake of your children, but secretly waiting for the whole thing to be over. Disillusioned by past Christmases, you bury your heart.

I've struggled with all these expectation attitudes: perfection, denial, and disillusion. I want a beautiful, clean Christmas, but it doesn't turn out. I want a peaceful, conflict-free Christmas, but someone messes it up. I try to harden myself against the festivities, pretending they don't matter, but my heart doesn't heal.

No matter what happens, I can't stop longing for a peaceful Christmas.

Christmas is a season with outrageous expectations. We expect much from ourselves. We expect much from our families. Our families expect much from us as well. The potential for disappointment is huge.

I am a recovering people-pleaser. In the years before my recovery, I wore myself ragged trying to please everyone at Christmas. Buying the perfect gifts, attending each event, pasting on a smile. Ironically, all my effort didn't produce peace—it seemed to escalate frustration and conflict.

With the help of wise Christian counsel, I learned my expectations were too high. I expected too much from myself—I can't please everyone. I expected too much out of my family—if someone had a meltdown, my Christmas wasn't automatically ruined.

God brought peace to my heart in my recovery years. He showed me that if I allowed myself to be led by the Holy Spirit through the challenges of the Christmas season, I would find life and peace.

God helped me adjust my expectations to include some brokenness, conflict, and disappointment. In time, I saw how leaving room for a little hurt opened up room for a lot more happiness and peace.

God also taught me to reorder my priorities, and when I did, my expectations fell into order.

I gained peace when I put God first in my day, listening for his direction and basking in his comfort, even during busy December.

I gained peace when I cared for myself with enough rest, exercise, and nutritious food.

I gained peace when I put the needs of my husband and children first before trying to please anyone else.

When my heart was settled in God's peace and my mind was led by his Spirit, I gained the peace that passes all understanding in the Christmas season.

How can your expectations be infused with God's peace this year?

<u>Day 3 Questions for Study and Reflection:</u>

Read Philippians 4:6-7. What are we instructed to do in verse 6 which leads us to peace in verse 7?

How can the peace that passes all understanding guard your heart and mind this season?

Which expectation attitude is most familiar to you? If none quite fit, describe a different expectation attitude you have toward Christmas.

List a few ways you can adjust your expectations on yourself. What expectations of others can you adjust this Christmas?

Day 4: Peaceful Words

For the mouth speaks what the heart is full of.
Matthew 12:34

Years ago, I learned the power of self-talk from my toddler son's rebuke.

On my drive home after small group Bible study, I mentally replayed my comments and began the familiar analysis of all I had shared.

In my mind, the self-talk track played: *You went too far. You shouldn't have said so much, you stupid girl.*

"Stupid is a bad word, Mama," I heard from the back seat.

Oh no—my inner voice had crossed my lips. I heard the harshness of the condemning word in his innocent voice.

"You're right, bubba. Silly is better. Mama's so silly."

My answer satisfied him, but I pondered it later during his naptime. I realized how often I practice negative self-talk, usually triggered by minor, everyday blunders. As I mentally reviewed common scenes which activate the harsh inner voice, I heard myself whisper leave me alone, leave me alone.

I asked myself, "Who needs to leave me alone—the great accuser Satan, or the harsh inner judge in my heart?" My answer: both.

I turned to the scripture we discussed that day in Bible study. Romans 8:1 stated there is no condemnation for me now, as a believer in Christ Jesus.

No condemnation for my sins long reconciled, my embarrassments long elapsed, my hurts long healed.

No condemnation for everyday mistakes, spills, blunders, and imperfections.

In God's grace, I found peace to quiet my harsh inner judge.

These days, the dark voice snarls less often. But when it accuses, *Do you know who you are?* I have my answer.

I no longer chant *bad, stupid, worthless.*

God's words of life resound:

I am redeemed (Psalm 71:23).

I am forgiven (Colossians 1:13-14).

I am chosen (1 Peter 2:9).

I am treasured (Deuteronomy 7:6).

I am protected (Psalm 37:28).

I am loved (Galatians 2:20).

I am his child (1 John 3:1).

I can speak peace to myself now because God's peace is my heart's overflow.

Learning to speak peaceful words to myself has helped me speak peace to others. I have learned to recognize the harsh, irritated, condemning tone of my inner judge. When that sharp edge comes out in my tone toward others, I remember how it feels to be wounded by words. I pause, acknowledge my wrong, ask forgiveness, and proceed with gentleness.

God has set peace on my tongue in place of condemnation. He has rehabilitated my heart as his peaceful dwelling place, and his peace has carried over into my speech. He can help you too if you desire to speak peaceful words to yourself and to others.

Day 4 Questions for Study and Reflection:

Read Romans 8:1-4. What price was paid so we no longer have condemnation before God?

Have you struggled with harsh self-talk? What have you done to stop the flow?

Read Matthew 12:34-37. How does this passage inspire you to change the way you speak to yourself and speak to others?

Choose one of God's words of life and look up the corresponding passage. In your own words, restate the verse so you have a ready answer for the accuser.

Day 5: Peaceful Actions

Blessed are the peacemakers,
for they will be called children of God.
Matthew 5:9

Think about all the people who will be affected by your actions this Christmas season.

People you know: Husband. Children. Family. Friends. Coworkers. Business associates. Pastors. Teachers. Hair stylist. Manicurist. And others.

People you don't know well: Sales clerks. Waiters and waitresses. Convenience store attendants. Delivery people. Strangers in line. Needy people. And others.

When you are impatient, will you snap words, sigh loudly, or leave the line in a huff? Or will you breathe deeply, focus your perspective, and offer a peaceful response?

When you are irritated, will you clench your jaw, give the stink eye, or grumble? Or will you pause, count to ten, and step back in peace?

When you are hesitant, will you avert your eyes, hide your smile, and walk away? Or will you step out in faith and make a connection?

I list all these examples because I've messed up so often. Too many times I've allowed my emotions to run wild in busy December, and I destroy peace rather than create it.

But I have a higher calling, and so do you.

As daughters of the Prince of Peace, we are called to be peacemakers.

Not only with people we know, but with everyone in our everyday lives.

In the past four days, we've discussed different aspects of a peaceful heart: peace with God, peace with ourselves, peaceful expectations, and peaceful words. Peace flows from the heart. Peaceful actions flow from a peaceful heart.

Before you write your shopping lists, plan your parties, and prep your recipes, will you think carefully about how to be a peacemaker this Christmas?

As a peacemaking mom, you can treat yourself well this season so you aren't running on empty. You can give your body the care it needs as a temple of God, so you can serve well.

As a peacemaking mom, you can show loving actions to your husband and children, creating special Christmas memories unique to your own home.

As a peacemaking mom, you can show honorable actions to family members, even if friction exists. You have God's power to change stressful gatherings with his peace.

As a peacemaking mom, you can show respect toward acquaintances and strangers, making the most of every opportunity. Perhaps you will introduce someone to the Prince of Peace this year.

Think about it: you may be the primary peacemaker in any given day to the people who cross your path.

You are an ambassador for the Prince of Peace.

You are the only one who can offer his gift of peace in your unique voice and spirit.

This Christmas season is your opportunity to serve all kinds of people with peaceful actions. We will discuss practical ways to serve in upcoming weeks. Will you choose now to be a peacemaker?

Day 5 Questions for Study and Reflection:

Read Matthew 5:1-12. Besides being a peacemaker, what other characteristics set you up to receive God's blessing? Which of these characteristics resonate with you right now?

When you look at the lists of people you know and people you don't know, which people on those lists need peace from you this year, and why?

When is it hardest for you to show peace through your actions?

What steps can you take to grow as a peacemaking mom?

Week 2: Peace in my Day

You will keep in perfect peace
those whose minds
are steadfast,
because they trust in you.
Isaiah 26:3

Day 6: Peaceful First Light

In the morning, Lord, you hear my voice; in the morning
I lay my requests before you and wait expectantly.
Psalm 5:3

What happens when you first wake up, before your feet hit the floor?

Do you hit the snooze button with a groan?

Do you check your smartphone for any messages or emails?

Do you begin the mental rundown of everything that must be done today?

I think those responses resonate with most moms. The breakneck morning pace begins before we even get out of bed.

I'm challenging you, as I'm challenging myself this season, to start the day off with God.

Before you even open your eyes, will you offer a prayer of thanks for another day to serve God and enjoy his creation?

Will you praise him as you brush your teeth and wash your face?

Will you ask him for peace as you get dressed?

Beginning the day with God will make all the difference between a peaceful season and a stressful season. It also prepares us to be better servants to our families, because our hearts are set right straight away.

For years I beat myself up about a lack of regular quiet time. When my babies were nursing and I ran low on sleep, meeting God early in the morning was difficult. Also, I used to juggle time on the treadmill and time with God before my children got up. I had the desire to meet God first, but carrying it out was so challenging.

Then I read a little booklet called <u>My Heart, Christ's Home</u>. This book painted the picture of Jesus waiting for me every morning. I imagined him sitting at my kitchen table. If I ran past him to eat, exercise, or clean the house, I tended to neglect quiet time with him the rest of the day.

I began praying, "God, please help me wake up and look forward to time just with you in the morning." When the alarm rang at 5:15 a.m. and I was tempted to rush, the Holy Spirit gently nudged, *"Remember when you prayed about this?"* So I went straight to the kitchen table, opened my One Year Bible, and started reading while my cup of tea brewed.

In these early morning meetings, I consistently hear God's messages louder than at any other time of day.

His Word comforts me. When I felt unappreciated, he uses 1 Corinthians 12:12-26 to remind me of my worth.

His Word corrects me. When I feel tempted to gossip, he reminds me of Psalm 141:3, when I read the passage and asked him to set a guard over my mouth.

His Word strengthens me. When I feel I can't give any more, he brings 2 Corinthians 12:9 to my mind, and I turn to him for grace in my weakness.

I use the rest of my morning prep time to pray. I pray aloud in the shower and on my commute to work after I drop my children off at school. I pray for his help and guidance in the rest of my day. I always feel better prepared for the day's stresses and more peaceful throughout my day when I have had that time alone with God first.

This season, when I join him in the mornings, I will be praying for you every day! I'm praying all of us will be filled with peace to carry us through our busy December days.

Day 6 Questions for Study and Reflection:

What is the most challenging part of early morning quiet time for you?

What changes are you willing to make to prioritize an early morning quiet time?

Read Psalm 143 and Psalm 145. What different themes do you notice in these two psalms? How could you incorporate those themes in your morning prayers?

How will morning quiet time help you become a peacemaking mom?

Day 7: Peaceful Mid-Morning

Because of the Lord's great love we are not consumed,
for his compassions never fail.
They are new every morning; great is your faithfulness.
Lamentations 3:22-23

It's 10:00 a.m. on a mid-December morning. What does your day look like?

When I was a work-from-home mom of little ones, I was already on my third load of laundry, thawing meat for supper, feeding a snack to my toddler while the baby napped, and working on a sales spreadsheet while considering gift ideas.

Now that I work outside the home, I'm usually eating a granola bar, estimating how many work tasks I can accomplish the rest of the day, deciding what to cook for supper, reviewing upcoming events in my planner, and checking over my shopping list.

If you're like me, you're fully immersed in mid-morning multitasking mode. This mode is a year-round necessity as a mom, but in busy December, it's life-or-death.

I don't know if you enjoy making lists, but for me lists are crucial to my peaceful outlook during busy December.

This is me without a list (ironically, in list form):

- Forgetting to purchase items I volunteered to bring to the class parties.
- Making last-minute stops for tape and gift tags, when everyone is crabby and tired.
- Scrambling to clean up the house before guests arrive because I didn't allot enough time earlier in the week.
- Staying up way too late on Christmas Eve to make the baby's Christmas stocking.

32

Not fun.

Not peaceful.

Our theme verse for this week states that God keeps us in perfect peace when our minds are steadfast due to our trust in him. My mind is steadfast when I trust God to provide for all my needs.

I trust him to help me serve my family. I trust him to help me carry out my tasks. I trust him to help me give thoughtfully and spend wisely. After much practice, mid-morning peace looks like this:

- A pleasant song playing in the background sets a peaceful mood. Listening to Christian music or Christmas songs helps me stay positive.
- A healthy snack of carbs plus protein helps me fight fatigue.
- My planner lays open to my daily list of tasks and events. I have stopped writing ideas on a million scraps of paper, which has cut chaos.
- I reserve one page for gift ideas, a list of retailers and coupons, and a gift budget. I reserve another page for new recipes, because I love baking Christmas cookies.

Looking over my lists mid-morning helps me prepare for the rest of the evening. I know if it's a night for a quick, easy dinner like chicken nuggets and veggies, or a night I can cook from scratch. I can see if I have time to shop or if it's better to use my time for cleaning. I can stay on task with my writing schedule by scheduling a daily writing hour. I don't stay on track as well without my lists, especially in busy December.

I remember best when I write everything down in a weekly/monthly calendar system. I use the Arc system from Staples, which is customizable and has plenty of room. You may prefer using your smartphone or another tool. Whatever method you prefer, I recommend you review it mid-morning every day.

This season, I'm using a specific planning method we will look at on Day 21. For now, I'm setting 10:00 a.m. as my daily review time so I can increase my peace through the rest of the day. I'm memorizing Isaiah 26:3 to keep my mind steadfast in busy December. Will you join me in a mid-morning review?

Day 7 Questions for Study and Reflection:

Read Lamentations 3:19-26. Who or what is the source of
Jeremiah's hope, and why?

Read Isaiah 33:2. What does Isaiah ask for every morning? How
can this prayer help you?

How might lists help you gain peace this busy December?

How might a mid-morning review help you as a peacemaking
mom?

Day 8: Peaceful Afternoon

May these words of my mouth and this meditation of my heart
be pleasing in your sight,
O Lord, my Rock and my Redeemer.
Psalm 19:14

I love the peaceful lull after lunchtime.

When my children were young and I worked from home, I made this a mandatory quiet time for everyone in the house. The younger children napped while my oldest child read. I went to my bedroom to read, write, or think. I needed a time of respite to reenergize for the evening ahead.

When I worked in an office I took my lunch into a quiet conference room and shut the door, getting the only silent fifteen minutes of my workday. I usually read a magazine or played a game on my tablet while I ate my salad.

This season, I'm trying something a little different in my afternoon lull with the goal of increasing peace in my heart.

I'm meditating on God's Word.

Surely you've heard the buzz about meditation. It's often suggested by experts as a stress reliever. Maybe you are wary of what seems a worldly, godless activity, and it can be.

When meditation centers on God's Word instead of self, it becomes a strengthening and peace-giving exercise. Like yoga for your heart.

Let's practice meditating on today's verse.

May the words of my mouth and the meditation of my heart
be pleasing in your sight,
O Lord, my Rock and my Redeemer.

I read this verse aloud several times, thinking about the most meaningful phrases. In this verse I focus on these words:

- words of my mouth
- meditation of my heart
- pleasing in your sight
- Lord
- Rock
- Redeemer

I break them down and apply them to my current situation, asking myself questions:

Which words of my mouth are pleasing to God? Which words are not pleasing to him? What is my heart meditating on today...where do my feelings keep circling? How can my heart's meditations please the Lord? In what ways do I need to submit to his rule as Lord of my life? How is he my Rock right now? How can I praise him for serving as my Redeemer in the past and in the present?

Finally I say the verse a few more times, locking the personal meaning in my mind.

Meditation on this verse will grant me peace because it centers me on God. It strengthens me because I am inspired to grow in character, and I am reminded of God's power. It gives me peace because I learn about God's powerful attributes, how he is bigger than any problem I face.

This verse will stick with me because I hide it inside my heart through meditation.

Meditation on a Bible verse takes only a little time in your afternoon lull. I've provided a free collection of verses for meditation in my online library. Sign up in the pink box at **sarahgeringer.com**. Use my verse collection for your meditation and watch your peace grow.

<u>Day 8 Questions for Study and Reflection:</u>

Read Psalm 119:97-105. How is meditating on God's law helpful in everyday life as a mom?

Read Psalm 119:148. Which of God's promises brings peace to your heart?

Take a few moments to read the beautiful Psalm 145. Which aspects of God's wonderful works in this psalm inspire you to praise God for what he's doing in your life?

In this busy December, how can your heart's meditations please the Lord?

Day 9: Peaceful Evening

Commit to the Lord whatever you do,
and he will establish your plans.
Proverbs 16:3

At the end of the day, I'm okay as long as I don't sit down.

Once I sit down, I'm done. I have no energy to do anything else.
Can you relate?

I have plopped down to watch an evening TV show, and got to
work late the next morning because I rushed to pack my lunch.

I have tumbled into bed without brushing my teeth and washing
my face, and I pay the price later with plaque buildup and
pimples.

I have fallen asleep before reviewing the kids' homework, and
the next day I sign permission forms at a stoplight on the drive to
school.

None of these are peace-producing results.

I have learned to get evening tasks accomplished while I'm still
standing. A little evening prep goes a long way toward a
peaceful morning.

When I know I will have a particularly busy evening, I try to take
a fifteen-minute nap between work and the event. Even if I don't
fall asleep, shutting my eyes and laying down helps me relax and
recharge.

On a normal evening, the most helpful steps I take are packing
lunch, choosing my outfit for the next day, taking a shower, and
checking homework papers. On the days I carry out one or more
of these prep projects, I see an immediate difference in the
morning peace level.

One new idea I'm trying this season is prepping breakfast. I have seen recipes for overnight oatmeal—simply soak oats in milk in the refrigerator, then heat in the morning, adding whatever toppings you like. That sounds like an easy, healthy, warm, and delicious breakfast on a cold December day. I also like to drink smoothies, and I can make sure my blender is ready to go and my ingredients are portioned the night before.

We will look at more meal prep ideas on Day 22. I'm excited to engage in conversation with you on my blog about your meal prep ideas and other ways you streamline your evenings to make mornings more peaceful.

I love today's verse because it holds such promise.

> *Commit to the Lord whatever you do,*
> *and he will establish your plans.*

God will reward me with success when I commit my plans to him. Even simple, everyday plans like managing evening tasks for the sake of a more peaceful morning matter to God, because he cares about my peace.

He wants me to bring peace to my home as a peacemaking mom. He wants my mind to remain steadfast because I trust him, and he wants to give me his peace.

I don't want December mornings to look like this anymore:

- Wasting ten minutes deciding what to wear
- Throwing lunches together when I need to be eating breakfast
- Helping one of my children practice spelling words while heading out the door

I want December mornings to be peace-filled so I can bless my family with peace as they begin their days. This seems possible only if I prep ahead the night before, while I'm still standing up. How can evening prep help multiply your peace?

Day 9 Questions for Study and Reflection:

Read Psalm 20:4 along with Psalm 37:4. How is your heart's desire linked to your plans?

Do you believe God cares about your everyday plans? Why or why not?

Which one step can you take this evening to make your mornings more peaceful?

Which one step can you teach your children to take tonight to increase peace?

Day 10: Peaceful Lights Out

Blessed is the one...whose delight is in the law of the Lord,
and who meditates on his law day and night.
Psalm 1:1-2

Lights out is much like first light.

If I begin and end my day with God, I have greater peace.

This season, I'm placing a special reminder by my bedside to meet with God at first light and lights out. You can download a free copy from my library by signing up in the pink box at **sarahgeringer.com**.

Years ago, part of my job was to run defragmentation on office computers. The program had a graphic which displayed the hard drive both before and after defragmentation. Before defragmentation, the graphic was a long, colored stream interrupted by lots of shaggy black lines, which represented the gaps. After defragmentation, the colored stream was almost seamless. The computers always ran more efficiently after this process.

I feel like a fragmented hard drive at the end of most days. All day I've faced stimuli and stressors which stretch me out, leaving lots of shaggy gaps in my peace.

Evening prayer defragments my day. God fills in the gaps with his grace and peace, helping my mind, soul, and spirit settle into a smoother stream and better sleep.

One tool I like to use is the ACTS prayer model—it stands for adoration, confession, thanksgiving, and supplication. Here's a peace-themed model for the ACTS prayer:

Adoration: Heavenly Father, I praise you because you sent Jesus to be my Prince of Peace. In Jesus I can find peace in abundant supply.

Confession: Lord, I admit to you the times today when I lacked peace in my heart. I hurt myself and others with my lack of peace in these ways: _____. I ask for your forgiveness. Please remind me to look to you for peace when I am tempted to stress out.

Thanksgiving: Today, Jesus, I thank you for granting me your peace in these areas: _____. Thank you for helping me grow as a peacemaker.

Supplication: Lord, I ask you to grant me peace in these ways: _____. I ask that you will help me serve others with your peace in this busy December.

Make this prayer your own every day, and watch how God fills in your shaggy gaps.

As today's verse states, lights out is also useful for meditation. You can incorporate your lunchtime meditation verse into lights out. Use a minute to glance over your daily meditation verse before you turn off the light. God will bring peace to your heart as you keep reviewing his Word throughout the day.

My sleep is more peaceful when I pray before falling asleep. Even if I drift off during prayer, I still have more peaceful rest. If I simply turn off the TV or close a book without checking in with God, my dreams are more scattered and my sleep is disrupted, and I start the next day with less peace.

When I wake in the middle of the night for no apparent reason, I consider that time an invitation to listen to God rather than a chance to review my to-do list. Often he brings matters to my attention I don't necessarily consider during the day: buried fears, unresolved conflicts, special insights. God uses those middle-of-the-night prayers to defragment the deepest parts of my heart and draw me closer to him.

How can you use lights out as a time to draw closer to God?

Day 10 Questions for Study and Reflection:

Read Psalm 19:1-6. How is nighttime associated with God's glory?

Read Psalm 19:7-11. How can this passage help you meditate on God's law at night?

Read Psalm 42:8. What Christmas song draws you close to God? How might you incorporate it into lights out?

What suggestion for nighttime prayer seems most helpful to you?

Week 3: Peace in my Relationships

If it is possible,
as far as it depends on you,
live at peace
with everyone.
Romans 12:18

Day 11: Peace in my Marriage

...in humility value others above yourselves,
not looking to your own interests
but each of you to the interests of others.
Philippians 2:3-4

As a newlywed, I had no problem prioritizing time with my husband during busy December. But when we became parents, busy December suddenly revolved around all the fun Christmas brings for children.

Each December my husband grew a little more Grinch-like. It took me a few years to recognize his grumpiness wasn't due to a dislike of Christmas, but because he missed me. I had been too wrapped up in special activities with our children and my regular Christmas tasks to notice.

We are both children of divorce, and our childhood Christmases were not usually peaceful. I learned that when I set time aside just for him during busy December, he feels valued and loved, and it's healing for both of us.

For the past several years we send the children to their grandparents' homes on Thanksgiving break. We enjoy several date nights of shopping, eating out, and watching movies. This Thanksgiving habit boosts the peace in our marriage at the perfect time, right before busy December sets in.

You know how hard it can be to squeeze in anything extra in December. The weekends are packed, and even the weeknights seem busier. But I have learned a date night between Thanksgiving break and Christmas vacation pays huge peace dividends in my marriage.

This year I'm scheduling a simple, inexpensive mid-December date with my husband. I won't bring up any holiday-related conflicts on this date. We won't discuss any heavy-hitting issues.

I will set out to create a peaceful memory with him and help him feel special.

We might go out for appetizers or a slice of cheesecake instead of a full meal. Maybe we will take a Sunday drive and watch for wildlife. We may go downtown to browse antique stores and people-watch, then take a walk by the river if it's not too chilly. Something easy, something relaxing, something peaceful.

Today's verse reminds me to focus not only on the parts of Christmas which interest me, but to what interests my husband. He isn't into Christmas concerts, parades, and decorating. What he likes best about Christmas is quality time with people he loves, most of all time alone with me. I am blessed to know that now, and that's why I work hard to reserve time only for him in busy December.

Take a moment to consider how your husband usually feels and behaves in busy December. Is it possible he misses you or feels left out? How can you look to his interests in this busy time? How can you carve out time just for the two of you? What can you do to help him feel special?

Get creative with a date idea and literally reserve a space for him in your December calendar. See if a few hours together, spent doing at least one activity he enjoys, increases your peace this year.

Day 11 Questions for Study and Reflection:

Read Philippians 2:1-11. How is Jesus' attitude a model for your marriage?

Read Ephesians 4:32-5:2. If you put these verses into practice in your marriage, how might your peace grow this Christmas?

What special Christmas food can you make or buy for your husband to let him know he's special?

What ideas do you have for a mid-December date?

Day 12: Peace with my Children

Fix these words of mine in your heart and minds...
Teach them to your children, talking about them
when you sit at home and when you walk along the road,
when you lie down and when you get up.
Deuteronomy 11:8-9

Christmas is the perfect season to teach your children about Jesus and peace.

First, though, let's talk about your heart again.

The past eleven days, we've been looking at ways to increase peace in your heart and attitude so it can overflow onto others. Your children know intuitively whether your heart is at peace through your words and actions.

Dear friend, I encourage you to purpose in your heart to create peaceful moments with your children this Christmas. Not perfect moments, but peaceful moments. Moments when you intentionally introduce your children to the Prince of Peace.

So many methods and tools exist. I encourage you to choose ones that fit your needs. Here are the ones which have helped me most.

When our children were small, we bought a toy nativity set for them. With this set they acted out the Christmas story in their own imagination, and they delighted in setting animals around the scene and placing baby Jesus in the manger. Times of free play with those toys planted seeds of the true Christmas story in their hearts.

I bought many Christmas picture books for their enjoyment. So many books feature the fun, light, playful aspects of the season, but I made sure to introduce them to stories about the Prince of Peace. Here is a list of their favorites:

Board Books:

"Who is Coming to Our House?" written by Joseph Slate, illustrated by Ashley Wolff

"What is Christmas?" written by Michelle Medlock Adams, illustrated by Amy Wummer

Picture Books:

"The Christmas Story" written by Patricia A. Pingry, illustrated by Wendy Edelson

"One Wintry Night" written by Ruth Bell Graham, illustrated by Richard Jesse Watson

"The Christmas Miracle of Jonathan Toomey" written by Susan Wojciechowski, illustrated by P.J. Lynch

"The Nativity" written and illustrated by Francesca Crespi (this is a beautiful pop-up book!)

This year since my children are at the age they enjoy longer stories, we will use Ann Voskamp's gorgeously written and illustrated "Unwrapping the Greatest Gift" in family devotions. I have found that even my tween son still enjoys read-aloud family time, and your older children may also.

Which books from your family collection serve as tools for teaching your children the Christmas story?

My children love Advent calendars. I use this one: "The Story of Christmas Story Book Set and Advent Calendar" written by Mary Packard and illustrated by Carolyn Croll. This is an imaginative retelling of the Christmas story in 24 little books ready to hang on a tree.

Over breakfast, we read the short daily story and they take turns decorating a small tree in our kitchen meant just for these little books. I like this resource because it keeps all of us in touch with the true Christmas story on a daily basis.

We often use the story of the day as a springboard for discussion on our drive to school and work. It's an easy way for us to start the day together in God's Word in busy December.

Please use these resources as inspiration for your own teaching toolbox, and make the most of your opportunities to speak about the Prince of Peace with your children this season.

<u>Day 12 Questions for Study and Reflection:</u>

Read Deuteronomy 4:9 and Joel 1:3. Why is sharing the true Christmas story with your children so important?

Read Proverbs 31:26-29. What reward awaits a mother who speaks to her children with faithful instruction?

When is the best time of day for you to teach God's word to your children? What methods work best for you?

What Jesus-centered activity can you do with your children this Christmas?

Day 13: Peace with my Extended Family

Let the peace of Christ rule in your hearts,
since as members of one body
you were called to peace.
Colossians 3:15

The first Christmas story includes a story about extended family.

When Mary found out she was pregnant, she went to her relative
Elizabeth's home. Elizabeth was near the end of her own
pregnancy. These two relatives in miraculous circumstances
gained peace and joy from one another's company.

When Jesus was born and the shepherds visited the baby, Mary
treasured up all the events and stored them in her heart (Luke
2:19). I imagine she added those events to the existing treasures
in her heart from her time with Elizabeth. Her time with
extended family likely strengthened and prepared her for the
challenging circumstances of Jesus' birth.

Time with relatives during Christmas is often a joy, blessing, and
source of strength. It can be a refueling of peace.

Time with relatives during Christmas can also be a challenge and
an opportunity to spread peace to people who are difficult.

One summer several years ago, a member of my extended family
caused a horrible scene at a large family gathering. This person
embarrassed everyone, but hurt one relative in particular. The
potential for a long-lasting rift increased as time passed.

At Thanksgiving that year, the hurt relative made an intentional
effort to greet the offender as soon as they arrived, welcoming
and embracing them in a humble yet grand display of peace.
This led to healing in the family and a surprisingly peaceful
Christmas.

Peace in our extended families is possible at Christmas, but it isn't possible without Jesus, and it isn't possible without intent.

If you set out early in December with the commitment to let the peace of Christ rule in your heart, you will be a peacemaker instead of a peace-disrupter at family Christmas gatherings.

Irritating words will turn into moments to breathe deeply in God's peace.

Offending actions will become opportunities to take the high road of peace.

Conflicts will become stages for peacemaking.

I have asked God to show me my part in past Christmas strife. When I have taken responsibility for my poor attitudes and actions, I have recognized the power of one person's ability to affect Christmas gatherings, for better or for worse. I want to have a heart filled with God's peace before I step foot into family gatherings this year.

God will give us hearts of peace so we will be attuned to the peace-seekers in our extended families. Maybe someone needs practical help, a listening ear, or a promise of faithful prayer. Maybe someone in your family is desperate for the words of peace only you can share in your unique voice.

I imagine Mary must have searched for the peace Elizabeth could uniquely provide from the bond they shared as family members. I imagine their time together solidified Mary's faith that God would provide a way through what seemed impossible.

Remember you are called to peace; you were not set in your family by accident, but you are called to be a peacemaker in the unique family God gave you.

This Christmas, will you purpose in your heart to bring peace to your extended family? Will you allow the peace of Christ to rule in your heart so it can overflow to all your family members, even onto the difficult people? Will you choose peace over conflict so you can point your relatives to the Prince of Peace?

<u>Day 13 Questions for Study and Reflection:</u>

Read Luke 1. What stands out to you about the relationship between Mary and Elizabeth?

Which family member refuels your peace? How can you offer special thanks to that person this year?

Read Colossians 3:12-17. How does this passage inspire you to treat your relatives differently this Christmas?

Which family member needs your peace? In what ways can you prepare your heart to offer them peace this Christmas?

Day 14: Peace in my Friendships

A friend loves at all times.
Proverbs 17:17

In busy December, my friendships tend to fall to the wayside unless I make intentional efforts to stay in touch.

The years I have made time for friends, I find a wellspring of peace which carries me through the challenges.

I am blessed with a special friendship which has lasted over 30 years. My dear friend has witnessed so many of my highs and lows and shares godly wisdom and insight like no one else. In busy December, her words grant me special peace.

The past few years, we have attended local craft shows together the weekend before Thanksgiving. This is a fun, relaxing time for both of us before busy December ensues. A few years ago, we both chose custom charm necklaces from one of the craft vendors, and it reminded us of girlhood fun in third grade. Pure joy, pure peace.

We talk for hours and hours over cheeseburgers and ice cream. She downloads her stories and I download mine, and we help each other process the junk. We give each other ideas for moving forward, and both of us leave the weekend with a treasure trove of peace to power us through Christmas.

Time with my dear friend before Christmas is major therapy for me. When I feel anxious or confused, I recall her advice. When I become irritated with the same old issues, I remember her wise words. She inspires me to choose a peaceful path.

Another friend of mine has a sunny personality. When I make the effort to call her even in busy December, I gain a bright spot of peace in the midst of my busy schedule. She reminds me of the joy of Christmas and the peace available only through the Prince of Peace.

When my children were younger, I met weekly with friends at Bible studies or by walking together. Now that my children are in school and I'm working, it's more challenging to meet with friends in person. I must schedule time for friends in advance or it simply doesn't happen. I find it easier to stay in touch on the phone rather than go out for girls' night this time of year.

This December, I'm planning to call one friend per week while I do housework or walk on my treadmill. I want to see how setting aside more time for friends increases my peace in this season. I want to show my friends love at all times, even in busy December, by carving out time for our relationships.

Do you tend to let friendships fall to the wayside during busy December? What can you do differently this year to cultivate your friendships? How might your peace increase if you reach out to your friends?

Day 14 Questions for Study and Reflection:

Skim over 1 Samuel 18-20. How was Jonathan the model of a friend who loves at all times?

How does the friendship between David and Jonathan inspire you in your friendships?

Which friend serves as a wellspring of peace for you? Why?

Which friend needs your peace this Christmas? What action can you take this week to share your peace with this friend?

Day 15: Peace in Work Relationships

Seek peace and pursue it.
Psalm 34:14

You can always promote peace in your workplace, no matter the situation.

Maybe you work in a stressful environment...maybe December is your busiest month. How can you serve as a peacemaker among others who are also under so much stress, whether they are co-workers or customers?

Maybe you work with one person who continually disrupts peace. Maybe they single you out; maybe they spread dissent wide and far. How can you handle the situations they create with peace this year?

Maybe you want to speak about the Prince of Peace with your co-workers. What can you do to lay a foundation of peace with them, so they are willing to hear what you have to say?

How can you intentionally promote peace in your work relationships?

I have learned to promote peace by listening to people's stories. I slow down enough to look them in the eye, search for the feelings underneath their words, and affirm their heart. They won't know me as a peacemaker unless I care.

I can promote peace when I operate as a team member. Whether it's refilling paper in the copy machine or cleaning another's mess without grumbling, I have learned to promote a peaceful environment by showing humility.

This one is especially difficult for me: I promote peace by keeping my words under control. Whether it's biting my tongue when I'm tempted to strike back, or counting to ten when a challenging customer pushes my irritation buttons, I have learned to be a peacemaker when I practice self-control.

Making an effort to connect also promotes peace. Maybe it's time for me to engage in real conversation rather than simply saying hello or talking about the weather. Maybe it's time for me to reach out to a struggling co-worker instead of ignoring the signs. When we take the risk to engage, we are peacemakers. Depend on the Holy Spirit to reveal when you need to engage.

Today's verse encourages us to actively seek peace. In a work environment, peacemakers create a better atmosphere for everyone. When I worked as a high school secretary, I had the potential to spread peace among all these groups:

- Co-workers
- Students
- Parents and grandparents
- School supporters
- Coaches
- Delivery people
- College and military recruiters
- Photographers
- Salespeople
- and more!

I had the opportunity to serve as a peacemaker among literally hundreds of people every day. All these groups need to see the Prince of Peace in this season. If I don't actively seek peace in my interactions with them, I miss out on the chance to point them to Jesus.

Think about the people you interact with at work—all the people who need the peace you can give this busy December. How can you purpose in your heart to bring them peace?

<u>Day 15 Questions for Study and Reflection:</u>

Read Colossians 3:23-24. How does God view your work? How does this passage affect your view of work?

Read Matthew 9:35-38. In light of this passage, how do you see yourself as a worker for peace?

Which work situation calls for you to be a peacemaker right now?

If you are a stay-at-home mom, how can you serve as a peacemaker in your work at home?

Week 4: Peace in my Surroundings

Peacemakers who sow
in peace
raise a harvest
of righteousness.
James 3:18

Day 16: Peace at Home

She watches over the affairs of her household
and does not eat the bread of idleness.
Proverbs 31:27

Dear friend, you have such great power to create a peaceful atmosphere in your home.

On Day 3 we talked about peaceful expectations. You can create a peaceful atmosphere by accepting that some ornaments might get broken, some recipes may not turn out, and some days may be marred by frustration and arguments. With peaceful expectations, words, and actions, you can expect wonderfully imperfect family memories this busy December.

You can create family memories which don't involve a lot of planning or expense. Our family likes the simple tradition of watching classic Christmas specials while drinking hot cocoa. For one night, I allow my children to pile on as many marshmallows as they wish.

My children like to use Halloween candy to create their own gingerbread houses. I use leftover cracker boxes and tape to create a house-shaped base. They use a can of white icing as glue for graham cracker siding and candy décor. I snip a hole in the corner of a plastic bag filled with icing, and they finish the houses with piped-on icicles. My children love this creative activity which costs only a few dollars and doesn't require a lot of effort.

On day 4 we talked about peaceful words. When God's peace fills your heart, you can let it flow over onto your husband and children.

Consider the times your words have disrupted the peace. Recently I felt frustration rise when I asked my son three times to do a chore, and I found it unfinished. Before I snapped at him,

I paused. I knew I had disrupted peace in our home too many times before by snapping in anger.

When I stopped to consider the situation, I realized he may have become overwhelmed since I asked him to do several chores at once. He's only ten years old, after all. I decided to calmly remind him one more time before giving a consequence. When I asked again, he finished the chore without incident. In this brief, everyday moment, I realized the power my words hold to create a safe haven of peace in our home.

On day 5 we talked about peaceful actions. Christmas is a fun season to create a peaceful home atmosphere in celebration of the Prince of Peace with simple actions. Here are ideas I use at Christmas.

I use scents to create peaceful memories. What scent brings you back to childhood Christmases? When I smell freshly cut cedar, I'm transported to my great-grandparents' sitting room and the happy Christmases in their home. Think of which scents you want your family to connect with peaceful Christmases in your home. If you don't want an open flame or hot wax from candles, you can simmer orange slices and cinnamon sticks in water on the stovetop. We have an artificial Christmas tree, so I use cedar-scented wax in my wax burner instead.

I like to place something special in my children's rooms to remind them of Christmas. They each have their own small personalized tree in their bedrooms, and I use timers for the lights so they can fall asleep while admiring the beauty. Also, I put something special in their bathrooms: fresh greenery from our woods, snowman towels, or scented hand-soap, so the Christmas spirit is in every room.

For my husband, I try to stay on top of the extra messes busy December brings. I combine my tasks by talking on the phone while cleaning up; I don't stop moving when I'm on the phone. I also try to quickly clean up after myself when baking or decorating, since I typically get lost in the fun and overlook the need to wrap up each project before beginning another.

Christmas is a perfect time to help everyone feel special with your actions. I make each family member their favorite cookie they eat only at Christmas. Then they have their own tin of cookies to snack on while watching Christmas movies.

Today's verse hints at the power you possess to set the tone in your household. When you are engaged and actively planning for peace, everyone will have peaceful memories of home.

Peacemakers will sow a harvest of righteousness. What harvest will you sow this year?

Day 16 Questions for Study and Reflection:

Read Proverbs 31:10-31. What initial emotion does this picture of a wife and mother stir in you?

Which actions of the Proverbs 31 wife inspire you to create peace in your home?

What reward awaits a mom with noble character (which includes peacemaking)? See verses 10-11 and 28-31 for your answer.

Which ideas will you apply from today's lesson to bring peace to your home?

Day 17: Peace at Church

The Lord bless you and keep you;
the Lord make his face shine upon you and be gracious to you;
the Lord turn his face toward you and give you peace.
Numbers 6:24-26

I love to see my church decorated so beautifully for Christmas, and I so appreciate those who pull it off every year since I hate climbing ladders! The poinsettias, garlands, and white string lights create a beautiful, welcoming, peaceful atmosphere.

Much more importantly, church is my primary power source for peace in busy December. I am drawn back to the real meaning of Christmas as I sit at the Prince of Peace's feet during Sunday worship. At the benediction (today's verse), I hear God's peace spoken over me. Worship in the company of others always settles peace deeply in my heart.

Mid-week Advent services are a special blessing. Yes, they add one more item to my busy December to-do list. However, these extra services keep my family centered on the true meaning of Christmas when materialism entices us. After Advent services, we also receive the blessing of fellowship with multi-generational fellow members at the simple church suppers of chili or tacos.

Christmas wouldn't be the same without opportunities to serve others through our church. My family and I have enjoyed these fun acts of service in recent years:

Caroling to shut-ins. The faces of many elderly people lit up when they heard my children's voices, and I watched God's peace fill all our hearts.

Adopting an international student. We made friends with a German graduate student who didn't grow up going to church, and found great joy in worshipping the Prince of Peace together on Sundays during Advent.

Sending Christmas dinner and presents to a down-and-out family. My small group gathered food and gifts for an unemployed family of four, and received great blessing from giving.

Operation Christmas Child. Over the past several years my family has packed and shipped dozens of gift boxes and received several letters from children all around the world. This ministry is a wonderful way to introduce others to the Prince of Peace, and my children really love building their boxes.

I want our children to become adults who make church a big priority at Christmas. We take them to the family-oriented worship service on Christmas Eve, and they enjoy taking part in the impromptu nativity scene.

In the past two years, my oldest son has asked to attend the 11:00 p.m. service only with me. This special time together has brought my heart deep peace. I love seeing evidence that my adolescent son already values church at Christmas.

So many children are leaving the church once they grow up. Christmas is a perfect time to recommit your family to regular attendance, with extra worship times and service opportunities.

It's also a great time to use the readings and sermons to spark discussion at home. I think many children fall away from the church because parents don't initiate faith discussions. How do you engage your children at home after church services?

My church prints a worship folder with scripture readings and sermon discussion questions. Over family meals the following week, we discuss how to apply the scriptures and sermons to our daily lives. We keep these discussions brief and simple, and I try to take an informal approach.

I want our family discussions to naturally flow into faith discussions so my children have a model to follow in their own families someday.

Dear friend, you have great power to make church a central part of your family life, and to keep your children engaged in their faith. What will you do this year to gain peace from church so you can share it with others?

Day 17 Questions for Study and Reflection:

Read 1 Corinthians 12:12-31. Why is participating as a member of the body of Christ (the church) so important? What do you gain by participating? What can others gain from your participation?

Do you attend mid-week Advent services? If yes, how does doing so increase your peace? If no, how might doing so increase your peace?

What opportunities can you find in your church to serve others and spread God's peace this Christmas?

What new action can you take to engage your children in faith discussions, based on what they hear at church?

Day 18: Peace in the Marketplace

There is...joy for those who promote peace.
Proverbs 12:20b

We all face it in busy December...more time shopping.

I know many moms have switched to online purchases, but I also know every mom has more stops to make this time of year, no matter how well she plans.

It's your choice: will you be a peacemaker or a peace-buster? Will you choose to scatter seeds of peace everywhere you go, including the marketplace?

As we have discussed on previous days, your words and actions make all the difference in how your peace is distributed. This includes standing in line, interacting with cashiers and wait staff, and placing change in red kettles.

When you head out to market, pray first for opportunities to bless others with peace. God will open your eyes to people you may have never noticed before. People who are ready to receive your unique brand of peace are waiting for you in the marketplace.

Maybe God will place a stressed-out person in line beside you who is desperate for the words of peace you can give. You can listen and offer an encouraging word.

Maybe God will give you the chance to thank a weary clerk for their service, and offer peace instead of irritation if something goes wrong. You can stand out from others who are snippy and demanding in busy December.

Maybe God will introduce you to a lonely woman who cleans restrooms, and your acknowledgment will bless her day.

Think about the times you felt unnoticed or unappreciated, and what a kind word may have done to give you peace.

Maybe God will help you see the guy stocking produce who needs a moment of kindness from the peace you share. Everyone around us struggles with hidden problems—only God knows which stranger needs to hear the words of peace you share.

When you say "Merry Christmas," do you look in their eyes? Do you make a real connection, however brief, as an ambassador of the Prince of Peace?

I have learned that my smile is a gift of peace. So many others will rush by without acknowledging, without eye contact, without smiling. Simply looking into the eyes of the overlooked and offering a smile ushers peace into their busy Decembers. It's a small gift, but one I forget to give unless I'm intentional.

You can also leave peace behind you by writing a snippet of encouragement, or possibly one of your meditation verses, on a tip receipt. When I've done this, my heart sings with peace as I leave the restaurant, even though it only cost me a few extra seconds.

Ask your children to help you look for people in the marketplace who need your peace. Involve them in sharing peace, and pray with them about watching for opportunities. My children love feeling like they are on a treasure hunt of serving others.

You will find joy in promoting peace in the marketplace. What other ways can you bless people in the marketplace with peace?

Day 18 Questions for Study and Reflection:

Read 1 Corinthians 9:6-14 through the context of sowing seeds of peace in the marketplace. How does this passage encourage you to sow seeds?

What benefits await you for sowing seeds of peace, according to this passage?

Think about the places where you regularly shop. Think of a particular cashier or waitress. How can you bless their day with peace next time they serve you?

How can you involve your children in sharing peace in the marketplace?

Day 19: Peace at Parties

Now may the Lord of peace himself give you peace
at all times and in every way.
2 Thessalonians 3:16

Almost all of us will attend a party this Christmas where we will mingle with people we don't know all that well.

For me, this is my husband's work party. I know many of his employees, clients, and business associates, but I will see many others at the party I've never met before.

This year I want to leave them with an impression of peace.

As an introvert, I'm not all that excited about striking up conversation with strangers. But over the past few years, I've gained some experience which has helped me feel less awkward and has often led to great conversations. Here are my methods, and I hope they help you give others peace at parties:

I ask who's on the guest list. A few days before the party, I ask my husband who will attend. Then I feel more prepared beforehand, having a better idea of how many new people will be there. I ask him questions about the new people to gather conversation ideas.

I start a conversation with what I know. Last year I talked with people who had just settled into a custom home my husband built. I knew they were using the home as a hunting lodge on their family farm. This basic knowledge gave me lots of talking points with people I'd just met.

I ask lots of questions based on their answers. This leads to a long chain of conversation. We talked about their childhood in an area familiar to me, then about the places where they had moved, then about vacations I'd taken in those states. We talked about hunting and land development. The conversation rolled along nicely, thanks to lots of questions.

<u>I show genuine interest and listen carefully</u>. Christmas is a great time to help people relax into peace by allowing them to share their stories. So many people are looking for someone who will simply listen. By listening I learn so much about the people in my husband's world. As an added benefit, my conversation with my husband is enhanced by what I learn from these party conversations.

<u>I look for windows to share my faith</u>. I look at these opportunities at parties to get to know someone new and possibly share God's peace with them. When I talk about faith with people I've just met, I only talk about my own experience. I don't preach—I simply weave faith into what I'm already sharing.

I look for signs of openness before I bring up faith. If a window suddenly closes, I change the subject. If a window raises open, a truly wonderful conversation can begin. When I pray before I attend, I'm more aware of the open windows and less afraid to take chances in sharing my faith.

If the opportunities arise, I will speak to them about how this study has brought me peace in busy December. I want my life to show others peace is possible through Jesus. I want the peace he gives me to overflow onto others, and I hope parties will be yet another place I can put his peace on display.

What ways can you share God's peace at parties?

Day 19 Questions for Study and Reflection:

Read 2 Timothy 1:6-8. When speaking with others about faith, what heart attitude does God want from us?

How can the Holy Spirit help you when speaking to others about faith? See John 14:26.

Think about an upcoming party. Which person there needs your peace the most?

What can you share from this study with people who need Christmas peace?

Day 20: Peaceful Travel

*Stand firm then...with your feet fitted with the readiness
that comes from the gospel of peace.*
Ephesians 6:14-15

If you are traveling this December, don't forget to first lace up
your peace shoes.

Ephesians 6:10-18 describes the armor of God, and the shoes are
the delivery system of peace.

I spend only a few hours in the car traveling for Christmas, but I
still benefit from wearing my peace shoes.

My planning, attitude, and expectations set the tone for a
peaceful trip.

I plan ahead with a fresh oil change and air in the tires. One of
our children vacuums the van so our gifts and food packages stay
clean. I pack snacks, drinks, and crowd-pleasing DVDs, and I
make sure phones and tablets are charged the night before.
Most importantly, everyone uses the bathroom before we leave.

All of these activities promote peace at the time of departure,
especially because my husband likes to leave on time. I have
found that when I skip or overlook one or more of these basic
prep steps, peace is off-kilter.

If we are staying overnight, I have learned to pack a few extra
items which help stabilize my peace level. I have trouble falling
asleep in unfamiliar rooms. So, I pack a sleep mask, earplugs,
and my own pillow. These simple items grant me better sleep,
which makes me less cranky and more peaceful while traveling.

The highway is a prime arena for promoting peace. I check my
attitude before I sit behind the wheel. I try not to ride someone
else's bumper, since I don't want to cause them the same anxiety
I feel when I'm in that situation. If someone gets too close to my

bumper, I quickly get out of their way instead of getting irritated. I set the cruise control to the actual speed limit and experience peace from no anxiety about receiving a speeding ticket. You know I say this because I received one not too long ago, right?

Early in my marriage I saw travel time as a great opportunity for hours of conversation, since this is my primary love language. But I learned my husband doesn't necessarily view travel time the same way, and he often becomes overwhelmed with too much talk.

I have adjusted my expectations over the years. If he's willing to talk, we talk and it's great. If he's quiet, I no longer try to extract conversation, which stirs conflict. I use the time to pray, reflect, give thanks, and admire God's creation. Either way, it's a win for me because my expectations are lined up with reality.

You also have the opportunity to promote peaceful travel as a guest. In a hotel, you can leave a note for the cleaning staff, thanking them and wishing them peace. I love doing this because I hope it blesses people who must feel unappreciated and invisible.

At someone's home, you can ask about their house rules and their preferences: should you remove the sheets and towels and place them in the laundry room, or do they prefer to clean up? In their home you can find other ways to promote peace by sharing the workload at mealtimes and perhaps watching the children. Think of other ways you may serve others with peace when staying at someone's home.

Plan ahead for peaceful conversations at your travel destination. How will you deliver peace to the people you will meet, whether strangers or loved ones?

Wherever you go this Christmas, put on your peace shoes first, and remember the Prince of Peace's gospel—he has given you all the peace you need (John 14:27).

Day 20 Questions for Study and Reflection:

Read Ephesians 6:10-18. Besides peace shoes, what other spiritual armor will help you most this Christmas?

Read Ephesians 2:14-18. How does Jesus give us peace?

What attitudes do you need to change in order to have peaceful travel this year?

What expectations do you need to adjust so you can promote peace during travel?

Week 5: Peace in my Holiday

Glory to God in the highest,
and on earth
peace
to those on whom
his favor rests.
Luke 2:14

Day 21: Peaceful Planning

Lord, you establish peace for us; all that we have accomplished you have done for us.
Isaiah 26:12

We have come to the final week of our study on peace. This week will weave all the previous days together for a blessed week of peacemaking near Christmas.

On many previous days we have spoken about planning ahead. Planning helps create order for the abounding tasks in busy December. Even though we are now on Day 21, I hope you have already found planning helpful to your inner peace level.

This year I have made a promise to myself to conquer procrastination with planning. Procrastination is a familiar, toxic companion of mine. It destroys my peace by upsetting me right before big events. But if I tackle one regular task and one holiday task daily, I can wipe out December procrastination.

This promise means I won't get all my outdoor light displays up and the Christmas tree decorated on the same day, or maybe even the same weekend. Looks like it's time for me to adjust my expectations again. I hope this plan will give me cleaner rooms with beautiful décor. Usually I have one or the other, but not both. This year my promise should help me stay on task.

I am searching for make-ahead recipes which freeze well, especially cookie dough. My peace will multiply if I only need to thaw dough out, slice or roll, and bake in busy December since I did all the prep and cleanup in November.

I plan to create a customized shopping guide before Black Friday begins. I will dedicate a page in my planner for gift ideas. I will mark gifts off as they are purchased so I don't stress out about last-minute shopping, or make the mistake of buying too much.

I plan to wrap gifts as I buy them. Rather than using wrapping paper and tape, I will use tissue paper to cover the gifts with an attached gift receipt, then drop them into one designated gift bag per person. If I need more than one gift bag per person, I can easily adjust it later. I want to spend less time wrapping this year and more time enjoying peace with my family.

This year I plan to delegate more tasks to my children. They are able to help more at their current ages than in years past. They can do one task while I'm doing another. For example, I need to start asking them to put away clean dishes while I cook dinner every night, and vacuum on a regular basis. Teamwork will create a more peaceful December for all of us.

I'm thinking about cutting out peace-buster projects. What is your peace-busting project that needs to go? Christmas cards? Light displays? Cleaning up after a live tree? I'm thinking through what can go this year so I can experience more peace. If I miss it too much, I can always add it back in next year.

I'm planning ahead for cleanup and a day to myself; we will talk more about this in the next few days.

I'm planning ahead for peaceful conversations with several loved ones. I can avoid touchy subjects and move forward with peaceful subjects.

I'm planning to set aside my anxious feelings and dwell on the peace Jesus has established for me. I'm planning to reflect on all the ways he has worked through me this year, and to thank him for all he has accomplished in my life.

Which plans will bring you more peace this year, and which plans will also create peace for others in your world?

<u>Day 21 Questions for Study and Reflection:</u>

Read Psalm 20:4. What is the desire of your heart this Christmas? Which plans do you want to succeed the most?

Read Proverbs 16:3 and Proverbs 19:21. How do these verses tie together?

What particular aspect of busy December will benefit most from your planning?

What do you need to set aside to dwell on the peace Jesus has established for you?

Day 22: Peaceful Preparation

The fruit of righteousness will be peace.
Isaiah 32:17

Busy December is full of temptations to sabotage your health. I have sacrificed sleep, exercise, and mindful eating for shopping, wrapping, and celebrating. Year after year my January peace has been wrecked with extra pounds, fatigue, and a blown budget.

This year I resolve to prepare well for my health so my peace can stay intact.

To prepare for better sleep, I'm using my promise in Day 21 to prevent staying up late due to procrastination. When I get less than seven hours of sleep three days in a row, I'm guaranteed to get a cold. I can't prevent every cold from happening, but I can prevent my sleep-deprived cold with more planning. I plan to be in bed, lights out, by 9:30 p.m. nightly, no matter what.

To prepare for exercise, I will consult my little Fitbit friend daily. When too many days go by without reaching my 10,000 step goal, I feel an unpleasant shift in the fit of my pants and my energy level. I prepare myself to hop on my treadmill in late afternoons and again for ten minutes after supper to help with my energy levels and digestion. I set this as an appointment with myself, not to be broken unless I'm sick, at least five days per week.

To prepare for healthy eating and to save our budget from too many take-out meals, I use the cook once, eat twice method. It's amazing how quickly a meal comes together when key ingredients are precooked and frozen. Here's a partial list of favorite ideas using foods I prepare in advance, then freeze in meal-sized portions:

Ground beef with chopped onions becomes sloppy joes, burritos or tacos, cheeseburger macaroni, skillet stroganoff, shepherd's pie, chili, or spaghetti sauce...so many possibilities.

Roasted chicken turns into pot pie, chicken salads, various wraps, chicken noodle or tortilla soup, white bean chili, and enchiladas.

I make my own chicken or turkey stock from leftover bones. Homemade stock-based soups freeze very well. Soup is part of my favorite healthy lunch on winter afternoons.

Diced ham is perfect for fried rice, scalloped potatoes, breakfast hash, and pizza.

I use one day per month to mix up several batches of pizza dough and cook dozens of pancakes. These go in the freezer for many quick breakfasts and suppers.

You can find a complete list of my favorite cook once, eat twice ideas by signing up in the pink box at **sarahgeringer.com**. If you have quick, healthy meal ideas to share, please share them on my blog so many other busy moms can benefit!

Finally, in my quest for healthy eating in December, I prepare myself to enjoy only one Christmas cookie per day. This is difficult for a sweet-lover like me, but I slow down and savor each bite, closing my eyes to fully enjoy the textures and flavors.

I offset the extra cookie calories with my December daily regimen of smoothies, salads, and soups. I let myself enjoy special treats at Christmas celebrations, but I still eat plenty of veggies and fewer carbs in my daily routine.

I'm okay with gaining two or three pounds over Christmas break, but not ten extra pounds which has destroyed my peace in the past. Advance preparation helps me stay on track.

I see the results of all this healthful preparation as the peaceful fruit of righteousness. How do you feel about this? What steps can you take to make this busy December healthier?

Day 22 Questions for Study and Reflection:

Read Galatians 5:22-23. Which fruits of the Spirit will help you get through busy December?

How is self-control of your health the peaceful fruit of righteousness?

Which area of your health will benefit most from peaceful preparation this season?

Which particular temptations do you need to prepare in advance to avoid?

Day 23: Peaceful Celebration

For to us a child is born, to us a son is given,
and the government will be on his shoulders.
And he will be called
Wonderful Counselor, Mighty God,
Everlasting Father, Prince of Peace.
Isaiah 9:6

The time to celebrate the Prince of Peace's arrival will soon arrive!

All our December planning and preparation in our hearts and homes point toward Christmas Day. The joy of this day is based on the arrival of our Savior, who makes peace with God possible.

This is a day of praise. At first light on Christmas morning, reserve a few minutes of praise in your heart before your day begins. Thank God for sending Jesus to be your personal Savior and Lord.

This is a day of worship. How can you make Jesus central to your celebrations? Some years we have had a short family devotion time, reading aloud from Luke 2. One year we made a birthday cake, lit the candles, and sang Happy Birthday to Jesus—my children loved it! Find a way to intentionally worship Jesus as a family on Christmas Day.

If you are traveling on Christmas Day, use your travel time to focus on Jesus. We have played Christmas-themed Veggie Tales and What's in the Bible? DVDs for our children during Christmas morning travel, so the true story of Christmas is prevalent in their minds. I use the drive time to reflect on God's faithfulness over all my past Christmases, and I pray silently for peace at our destination. When I pray for peace at family gatherings, my eyes are opened to ways I can promote peace on Christmas Day.

Christmas Day is a day to live at peace. It's a day to take the high road. It's a day to give the gift of peace by disengaging from strife. You give this gift to yourself as well as others. As far as it depends on you, live at peace with everyone on Christmas Day.

Christmas Day is a day to speak peace. Pray that God will show you who needs to hear your words of peace this day. Listen for cues. Look for opportunities to share how this season has been different due to your focus on peace. People will listen to you when they feel loved, heard, and affirmed. Look for new ways to share God's peace with your loved ones, including those who may not yet know Jesus as their Prince of Peace.

Christmas Day is a day of peace and joy. Joy and peace are best friends. On Christmas Day, revel in the joy. Delight in your husband, your children, and your own joy of salvation. There is joy for those who promote peace. Take joy in all the ways God has helped you share peace in this season.

Glory to God in the highest, and on earth peace
to those on whom his favor rests.
Luke 2:14

At lights out, meditate on this verse, substituting your name for "those." Think about how God sent Jesus to be your peace long before you were born. Think about ways you can glorify God for giving you this gift.

Let the angels' Christmas song bring abiding peace to your heart.

Day 23 Questions for Study and Reflection:

Read Isaiah 9:2-7. What special name could you give God for what he's doing in your life now? Get creative...be inspired by the names here and come up with your own!

Read Luke 2:1-20. What part of the Christmas story brings you peace today?

This Christmas Day, how will you praise Jesus as your Prince of Peace?

This Christmas Day, how will you work to promote peace?

Day 24: Peaceful Cleanup

"Peace, peace to those far and near," says the Lord.
"And I will heal them."
Isaiah 57:19

After Christmas each year, I feel a little low after the natural seasonal high.

The low hits me on the morning of December 26, when I see all the new stuff covering my counters and floors. My desire to show thankfulness for gifts and blessings is sometimes overshadowed by a temptation to grumble about cleanup.

Yet God has shown me ways to make Christmas cleanup more peaceful over the years.

In the kitchen, I used to dread the task of handwashing dishes since it consumes so much time. Now I use this time to listen to Christian podcasts. My mind sits at the feet of the Prince of Peace, listening to his Word on my IPhone, while my hands wash cookie sheets and wooden spoons.

As I snip the tags off clothing and toys, I take note of the country where the items were created. I pray for the people who crafted the items, taking a moment to envision their plight, recalling news stories of poor people who work in foreign factories. I pray God will bless those people and lead them to a saving knowledge of Jesus. The act of praying for strangers around the world fills my heart with God's peace which passes all understanding.

When I gather up cardboard and plastic packaging for the recycling bin, I give thanks for each family member who gave us wonderful gifts. I remember conversations we had and I pray over their concerns. I ask God to bless them and give them his peace.

When I take down outdoor lighting, it's usually freezing cold. But I look out over the winter landscape and thank God for the subtle beauty of many shades of brown contrasted with the blue sky. I thank God that no winter lasts forever, and for the promise of new life in him.

When I pack away my Christmas tree ornaments, I thank God for his faithfulness. I look over the ornaments I collected as a teenage girl, and I remember how God was there with me in difficult times. I carefully handle ornaments we received as wedding gifts, and I thank God for standing with us throughout our marriage. I pack away ornaments purchased when my children were babies, and the ones they created in preschool. I thank God for all the growth I see in them and I pray for their futures.

To fill the void of no décor after so much Christmas beauty in my home, I switch my red and gold decorations to blue and white snowmen décor in January. The white lights help alleviate my winter blues, and the smiling snowmen faces remind me to look for joy in new beginnings, which God ordains for me each year.

Asking for help is another way cleanup grants me peace. Cleanup is not as overwhelming now that my children are older and able to take on cleaning tasks without much effort. Each year I delegate a few more age-appropriate tasks. This increases my peace and establishes a spirit of family teamwork. I hope by working as a team now, my children will carry peaceful cleanup into their own families someday.

God's peace heals me when I feel low after Christmas. God's peace fills me when I clean up with a right attitude. God's peace calms me when I enjoy a home restored to order.

Day 24 Questions for Study and Reflection:

Read Isaiah 57:14-21. What kind of spirit does God bless with peace?

Look at verse 19. What kind of healing do you need this season? How can God's peace help you heal?

Think of your most dreaded Christmas cleanup task. How can you transform this task into a time of praise, thankfulness, or prayer?

In what ways can you involve your children in peaceful cleanup after Christmas this year?

Day 25: Peaceful Reflection

You will go out in joy and be led forth in peace.
Isaiah 55:12

I give myself one day of Christmas break as a gift of peace.

My husband enjoys an afternoon with his buddies. My children enjoy an overnight visit with their grandparents. I spend the day not catching up on anything except sleep. The dishes and laundry can wait during my peaceful day.

In the morning, I visit Panera for a pumpkin muffie and hot Earl Grey tea with honey, two of my favorite treats. I browse the clearance racks at the mall for deals, taking time to look over beautiful things without feeling rushed. If I have any gift cards, I use them on this day. One year my husband gave me a gift certificate for a massage—now THAT was a peace-inducing afternoon!

If the weather is agreeable, I put on layers of warm clothing and head to the park for a walk in the winter sunshine. If the weather is too cold or icy, I hit the treadmill. During my walk, I reflect on all God's goodness to me, month by month, in the past year.

I thank him for walking with me in my trials. I remember his provision. I pray over all my concerns. I look forward into the following year and lay the future in God's hands. After this prayer walk I feel cleansed on the inside and out, and peace sweeps over me.

A day of reflection helps me take stock of what worked and what didn't work this Christmas. I make notes in my journal so I can carry forward good ideas into next year and discard ideas that don't work anymore. I make notes on which recipes worked and which recipes don't need repeating.

At the end of each year I write in my journal about God's faithfulness to me. On my day to myself I review old journals, marveling and sometimes weeping over how God worked in my life and revealed his plan day by day. This year I plan to reserve part of my peaceful day recording all the ways God helped me in my writing career.

My peaceful day ends with a relaxing shower and a night out on the town with my husband. This day rejuvenates me and refreshes my faith, serving as a fountain of peace for weeks to come.

I encourage you to give one day of Christmas break as a gift of peace to yourself. Write it on your calendar; make arrangements for your children ahead of time. Ask your husband to occupy himself for the day, then bless him with an evening together.

Prepare a list of treats to give yourself. Do something healthy, like eating light or taking a walk, along with something indulgent, like savoring a piece of high-quality chocolate or soaking in a perfumed bubble bath.

Plan a time of reflection and prayer. Use your time alone to look back on all God's blessings in the past year and reflect on his peace revealed to you this Christmas. Spend time alone with Jesus and let his peace flow over you.

Read Isaiah 55. Which verse in this chapter gives you peace? Why?

When you reflect on the past year, how have you gone out in joy? How will you be led forth in peace?

How might a day to yourself during Christmas break serve as a fountain of peace?

In what ways has this study ushered peace into your Christmas?

Peace Be With You

May the God of hope fill you with all joy and peace
as you trust in him, so that you may overflow with hope
by the power of the Holy Spirit.
Romans 15:13

I hope this study has blessed you with God's peace in a new way. I would love to hear how God has worked peace in your heart through this study. Please join my Facebook page at **facebook.com/sarahgeringercreates** and let me know how God brought you peace. I look forward to reading your comments!

Want more Christmas peace? You will find free printables, prayers, and videos for this book when you sign up in the pink box at **sarahgeringer.com**. You'll find lots of other free goodies in my library when you sign up.

Your review of this book on Amazon, Goodreads, and other social media will help others find peace. **Please take a few minutes to post an honest and helpful review.** I deeply appreciate your shares as I work to grow my writing ministry.

Suggest this book to a friend or family member who needs God's peace at Christmas. You never know whose life may be changed by spreading the word.

May God bless you as you seek a peaceful Christmas season!

Sarah Geringer

About the Author

Sarah Geringer is a devoted follower of Jesus, wife, working mother of three, and a writer and artist. She has blogged since 2010, and currently writes about Finding Peace in God's Word at **sarahgeringer.com**.

Sarah has always loved Bible study. As a child, she gained a strong foundation of Bible knowledge through Lutheran education. When Sarah became a mother, she found friendship, encouragement, and support through small group Bible study at her church. Check out her other two Bible studies: **Newness of Life**, based on Ecclesiastes 3:1-8, and **The Fruitful Life**, based on the fruits of the Spirit in Galatians 5:22-23.

Sarah holds a Bachelor of Arts in English from Covenant College and a Bachelor of Fine Arts in graphic design and illustration from Southeast Missouri State University. She enjoys reading, writing essays and poetry, drawing and painting, gardening, baking, scrapbooking, journaling, and walking in God's beautiful creation.

Sarah lives with her husband and three children in her beloved home state of Missouri.

Connect with Sarah at **sarahgeringer.com** and through these other online outlets:

Facebook: facebook.com/sarahgeringercreates

Pinterest: pinterest.com/s105

Twitter: twitter.com/sarahgeringer

Instagram: Instagram.com/sgeringer

Goodreads: goodreads.com/sarah_geringer

40842355R00057

Made in the USA
Columbia, SC
13 December 2018